Motivating the Disaffected

Complex Specific Learning Difficulties

Dr Gerald Lombard

Complex Specific Learning Difficulties

Published by Lifetime Careers Wiltshire, 7 Ascot Court, White Horse Business Park, Trowbridge BA14 0XA.

ISBN 1 902876 71 7

Printed by Cromwell Press, Trowbridge
Cover illustration by Russell Cobb
Text design by Ministry of Design

Motivating the Disaffected
Series editor: Dr Gerald Lombard

Complex Specific Learning Difficulties is one of a series of six titles designed to help professionals in education and advisory work to motivate and encourage students who are disengaged from learning.

Each book provides a concise and practical guide to topics that are of particular concern to teachers and advisers.

The other titles in the series are:

The ABC of Approach to Classroom Behaviour Management
Asperger Syndrome and high fuctioning autism:
        guidelines for education post 16
Motivational Triggers
Social Competency: reading other people
Staying Safe

To order copies, please contact Orca Book Services Ltd, Stanley House, 3 Fleets Lane, Poole, Dorset BH15 3AJ. Tel: 01202 665432. Fax: 01202 666219.

For further information about these and other products published by Lifetime Careers Publishing, please contact our customer services, tel: 01225 716023; email: sales@lifetime-publishing.co.uk, or
www.lifetime-publishing.co.uk

Dr Gerald Lombard, C. Psychol., AFBPsS

Ged is Director of The Independent Psychological Service, which is an intervention and training service for young people and adults. He primarily works with individuals who 'won't, can't or can't be arsed' (one client's view of their work).

As a Chartered Psychologist, his major areas of interest are motivational principles, social competency (reading faces with intent) and complex specific learning difficulties. Ged was a secondary school teacher for 15 years, a part-time tutor/psychologist at two prisons and has held his current post for over ten years.

Contents

cont'd

Introduction

The aim of this book is to provide a simple guide for complex specific learning difficulties (complex SpLD). The guide is intended primarily for youth professionals working with young people aged 13 years to 20 years but can also be relevant to younger and older individuals. It is accessible to young people and parents, but it is educators and trainers I really want to reach in this first attempt. I estimate that over 80% of the clients I meet have a complex SpLD profile.

It is important to state that this book is a personal perspective of complex SpLD, drawing on 25 years teaching experience including research and assessment work. Despite referring to empirical and scientific research, the words in this book are intended to help as a general overview. There remains a proliferation of findings in the area of complex SpLD – and I do not intend adding to these. My findings are the result of experience, readings, jottings and some extremely useful information gleaned from young people and colleagues. In other words, this is a brief perspective and guide. You may find some sections on aspects of SpLDs very short – this may be because many aspects will already have been covered in earlier sections, or because the approach is designed to be as simple as possible.

Finally, my best teachers in this area were a group of 10-year-olds at a residential school for specific learning difficulties (SpLD). Over a 12-month period they helped me realise that 'going with a thinking style' is more beneficial than imposing a programme of your own. More importantly, they helped me understand persistence, motivation and dignity in the learner. It is to those 10-year-olds (now in their thirties) that I thank for a superb education.

Complex SpLD or SpLD?

Well over two decades ago SpLD was generally thought to refer to dyslexia. However, once the research into dyslexia began in earnest, it was found that SpLD was far more complex than just dyslexia! Other related, but discrete, areas of 'difficulty' became more apparent, e.g. dyscalculia, dysgraphia, dyspraxia, and overlapping profiles or styles of thinking, e.g. Scotopic Sensitivity Syndrome, Attention Deficit Disorders and Asperger Syndrome, that had some elements of other SpLDs.

Therefore, several decades later, the view often preferred by practitioners is of a complex SpLD continuum with overlapping difficulties, differences and syndromes (see diagram 1.1).

Diagram 1.1: The complex SpLD continuum

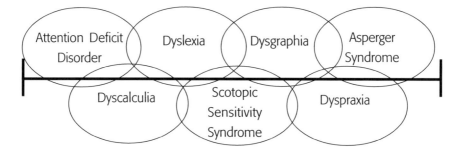

The continuum is intended to show that there are some similarities in the styles of perceiving and thinking and the difficulties experienced in the range of complex SpLDs. Also, these complex SpLDs may present in isolation, i.e. I experience Scotopic Sensitivity Syndrome but none of the other complex SpLDs, or they may co-exist, e.g. many learners with Attention Deficit Disorders also experience dyslexia. One young man I previously worked with experienced dyslexia, Attention Deficit Disorder with hyperactivity and Asperger Syndrome.*

* Asperger Syndrome and the autistic spectrum will not be covered in this publication – another book in this series *Asperger Syndrome and high functioning autism: guidelines for education post 16,* by Hilary Dinham, examines autistic spectrum disorders in post-16 education.

So, the term complex SpLD acknowledges the range of learning difficulties, and is not specific only to dyslexia. Therefore, if someone says to you: *'He/she has specific learning difficulties'* you should ask: *'Which ones?'* It could be SpLD/dyslexia, SpLD/dyscalculia, SpLD/dysgraphia, etc.

Let us begin by looking at the best known of the complex SpLDs: dyslexia.

Section 1
Dyslexia

How common is dyslexia?

Estimates vary from 4% (severely affected) to 10% (including those who are moderately and mildly affected) of the population. Some studies have claimed dyslexia rates of 17%, but these estimates have not been confirmed. My suspicion is that many continue to confuse weak literacy with dyslexia. The descriptions that follow will show that dyslexia is a *specific* difficulty, and not a difficulty that is general.

The rates of dyslexia in English-speaking countries (and French-speaking countries) remains at the 4-10% levels. However, in Italy, Germany, Finland and Holland the rates of dyslexia are much lower – sometimes as low as 1%. A popular myth is that these countries have more effective educational systems. Well, they may have – but it is not the reason for lower dyslexia rates! The major reason is that the written language in those countries is more regular phonetically, i.e. the words are often written as they sound. For example, what sound does the English spelling of the word psychology begin with? An 's' sound, yet the first letter is a 'p'. Now take the words *bow, bough, rough, right*? Where is the regularity of the sounds in these English words? Therefore, English and French written language is frequently irregular. A more phonetically regular spelling of *psychologist* would be *sikolojist* – and this is where many European written languages have the advantage. More regular spellings do not disadvantage as many learners who have a phonetic processing problem, i.e. problems learning their phonic sounds. If you have a phonetic learning problem, (even if you eventually learn all the phonic sounds), you can still frequently have trouble with syllables within words.

The complexity of the English and French written language is likely to date back to texts written in the 12th and 13th centuries by the aristocracy and clergy in England and France. To avoid ordinary people like you and I learning to read, the text was written in a type of secret code – at least, difficult enough to decode without some expert teaching. This gradually reduced over several hundred years, especially when the printing press was introduced, which made reading available to a wider audience. However, there remained many elements of the early complex codes of written language – and as we know, they still remain.

However, in China and Japan there are considerably less problems with dyslexia in their educational systems. The reasons for this will become more evident later, but it is enough to say at this stage that dyslexia does not interfere significantly with their written languages – phonics do not play a part. The word for *psychologist* will be a picture or symbol in Chinese or Japanese, thus overcoming the problem of pronouncing or encoding (spelling) sounds as syllables within words. The rate for dyslexia in Chinese and Japanese education is nil – yet they still have students who would have problems with phonics, or confuse left and right, or have memory problems.

So, is dyslexia a medical problem? Is the dyslexic person damaged in some way? As we will discover, individuals with dyslexia have specific thinking and learning styles, and have a brain physiology slightly different to individuals without dyslexia. Therefore, dyslexia is not a medical problem – we cause it to be an educational, social and emotional problem because we do not accommodate this thinking and learning difference.

Can you see dyslexia?

It is often described as 'the hidden difficulty' because people cannot see dyslexia by just looking at somebody. Physiologically, it is well hidden inside the brain. In non-dyslexic brains, the symmetrical plana (which is a structure in both the right and left hemispheres of the brain) is the same size in *both* hemispheres, hence the use of the word symmetrical. In dyslexic brains, this structure is asymmetrical – there is a difference in the size of the plana in one hemisphere. In some dyslexics, there are also some differences in the messages sent from the retina to the visual cortex (this is known as the magnocellular system). These physiological differences can cause phonological problems with written language and/or visual processing problems of words on a page. However, they do not affect accuracy of hearing sound (auditory acuity) or being able to perceive accurately an object or picture (visual acuity).

Now stop worrying – that is as far as I am going to go on the gobbledegook of psycho-physiology babble!

Does dyslexia run in families?

In general, yes. Recent studies, which have been investigating what gene is responsible for what behaviour, have estimated there is an 87% genetic loading with dyslexia, i.e. it is 87% likely that someone with dyslexia has someone else in their family with dyslexia. Also, it can occasionally jump a generation (i.e. no-one in the immediate family may have dyslexia, but grandad or grandma did, or a cousin or uncle may have dyslexia).

So how do you see dyslexia?

This is often hidden until the young learner begins school. Here are some key signs in five- to seven-year-olds:

1.   Evidence of early speech problems, i.e. difficulties in pronouncing words correctly, or getting words in the right sequence. A speech and

language therapist may be required to help the child with these early difficulties. Despite these early pronunciation problems with speech sounds, children can still have a wide vocabulary, express their views clearly and articulately, and appear bright in their understanding of others' language.

2. Difficulty in hearing the difference of similar phonic sounds, e.g. b/p/d and g/j and u/y/l and f/v/th (note: phonic sound is best remembered as the sound at the beginning of a word, such as the 'b' sound in 'bread', or 'j' sound in 'jug' or 'y' sound in 'yacht' – there's another example of good English spelling!

3. Learning and remembering auditory patterns may be difficult, e.g. the sing-along alphabet (did you learn your alphabet by singing the 26 letters?), times tables (did you learn your times tables by chanting the sequence?), not being able to recognise rhyme (that 'dog' rhymes with 'log', that 'cat' rhymes with 'hat').

4. Lack of concentration and attention when spoken to, and a lack of interest if stories are read.

5. Weak fine motor skills – often unable to keep within the lines when colouring pictures and problems when using scissors and pencils.

6. Development appears normal, but lack of progress in reading, writing and spelling.

7. Difficulty when forming letters onto a page, perhaps evidence of mirror writing, frequent confusion with b/d, p/g, j/u/y, m/n and s/z.

8. Cannot see the logic in the pronunciation of some words written in front of them – will argue that the word is not pronounced like that.

9. No sense of left and right.

10. Has trouble deciding which hand to use for fork, knife, spoon, or which hand to use to catch a ball, or which hand to use for drawing.

11. Poor gross motor control (legs/arms) when moving – appears clumsy.

12. Cannot remember instructions – forgets a sequence of instructions very quickly and may only remember the first part of the instruction, e.g. 'Go into the kitchen and get the milk out of the fridge'... may result in the child standing in the kitchen but not knowing what to do next!

13. Cannot remember their home address, or birthday, or the day of the week it is, or have real difficulty learning to tell the time.

14. Use their fingers (or counters/beads) to count simple calculations.

15. Difficulty in playing sequencing and matching games. This may result in frustration when playing games because 'they never seem to take their turn' or 'know when it is their turn.'

16. Problems doing up buttons, zips, tying shoe laces, and with the order in which they put their clothes on.

17. Tantrums and signs of frustration at home – and at school – for no apparent explanation.

18. Daydreaming and switching off in class and at home.

19. Reluctance to go to school after a happy start.

20. Literacy problems have already occurred in the family.

NB. If ten of these indicators are evident, then the young child is 'at risk' of experiencing educational difficulties, and it should be brought to the attention of the Headteacher. The more indicators above ten, the greater the likely level of severity.

Can you see these signs of dyslexia in teenagers and adults?

Yes, the above indicators have residual effects into older years. Individuals with dyslexia are often brighter than the average (one study cited that dyslexics have an IQ 1.7 points higher on average than non-dyslexics).

Unfortunately they are frequently unable to demonstrate their true ability because of *written* assessments and tests. However, they can and do learn strategies to help overcome many of the problems they face, or mask their difficulties by overlearning or finding a way around it.

For example, look again at point 3 in the previous list (problems remembering rhymes). Many adults with dyslexia cannot recall the rhyme '30 days hath September, April, June and November all the rest have 31, except February alone, which has 28 days and 29 each leap year.' However, they are able to recall the number of days in a month using a visual and practical strategy (see diagram 1.2)

Diagram 1.2:

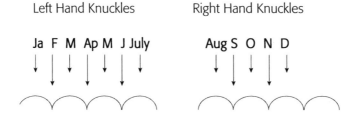

The rule is: wherever there is a knuckle, that will be 31 days, between knuckles is 30 days or less. So all you need to know now is the 12 months of the year (January to December) and that February is the strange month of 28/29 days.

Now looking at point 1 in the previous list: adults may have experienced early speech problems that are not noticeable in adulthood but continue to have difficulties pronouncing words like specific (comes out as pacific), or statistical (comes out as satitical). Often, the strategy used by them is to use an alternative word, or make a joke about their teeth needing to be fixed. My dad, a wise and clever man with many dyslexia indicators, could never say 'Coca-cola', it always came out as 'Coca-loco'. So he called all fizzy drinks 'lemonade' (in a red can, or yellow bottle, etc), because he could pronounce lemonade.

The indicator in point 2 in the list can still be observed by reading errors (e.g. *spilt* read as *split*), i.e. they may have learned to read reasonably well but certain sound combinations in words can undermine them. Often this results in a slower than expected reading rate. It is not accurate to assume that individuals with dyslexia are poor readers. Some dyslexics can successfully read every word on a reading test, or understand written text given to them. However, it is likely they experienced some early problems with reading and the only indicator now is a slow reading rate. It is also important to note that some individuals have developed perfect reading skills whereas others may still struggle to read a tabloid newspaper. So the indicator in point 6 (normal development but lack of progress in reading, writing and spelling) may now be relevant to only encoding (writing) language and not decoding language, or it may remain with reading problems only, or all three.

With the indicator in point 4 in the list, listening to stories or being spoken to, may no longer present as a problem – but being spoken at in lectures is likely to be dire for many. A teaching approach that is visual, kinaesthetic (doing, moving) and auditory (being spoken to) is more likely to succeed – purely auditory presentations can be torture and unhelpful for many with dyslexia.

With the indicators in points 5 and 11 many adults still describe themselves as 'cack-handed', but once they know where their learning strengths are, they accentuate what they can do. This can hide any continued fine motor problems, although holding a pen or handwriting can often remain a problem for many. So give them a laptop computer!

Earlier directional confusions can apparently disappear for many. However, despite fluent responses to left/right orientations, confusion can occur if asked to respond from another's point of view, e.g. *'With your right hand point to my left ear.'* Then, the old confusions of direction and laterality (sidedness) re-occur (as in indicators in points 9 and 10).

Developing a dominant side can be very important in directionality. For example, I am right-eye and right-ear dominant, right-hand and right-foot dominant – right-side dominant. I have no problems with directionality. However, if an individual is left-handed, they enter very much a right-handed world. I have a fine motor tendency to write from left to right, but a left-hander has a motor tendency to write from right to left on the page. Then, when writing in the *required* direction, a left-hander will obscure the line of text as writing ensues, thus taking away some continuity of experience. Sometimes a left-hander will also be left-eye dominant, and will visually scan written material from right to left. Consequently, spelling patterns become disturbed as well as the order of words in a sentence. This can result in difficulties with the fluency of reading and writing in general.

The worst approach one can make with someone with left-side laterality is to seek to change them to a right-hand mode – it can often lead to confused laterality and unnecessary educational and emotional problems. Once past the age of seven, learners should be encouraged to develop a preferred side and learn how to deal with everyday routines (see 'Do's and don'ts' later).

Many individuals with dyslexia develop ambidextrousness or mixed laterality, i.e. left-eye and left-ear dominant, can use both hands equally effectively, and right-foot dominant. The key here is to acknowledge positive differences and support whenever necessary.

Indicators in points 7 and 8 can be observed in long hesitations when writing similar letters (b/d), or being unable to tell the difference between the phonic sound/symbol or u/y. I continue to have many conversations with clients about the English language's bizarre spelling – not their bizarre spellings. Frequently, I have to agree with their logic as I watch them crossing out another word that does not look correct to them.

Indicators in points 12 and 13 and 14 often remain but tend to present themselves as disorganisation, late arrival or non-arrival. I work with a talented colleague who experiences dyslexia and exhibits all three indicators. For him a palm top computer combined with telephone and dictaphone has transformed his memory, recall of information, calculation skills, and (worst of all) trumpeting his colleagues' late arrivals for meetings! When in meetings, a little bleep reminds him that he should leave soon for his next appointment. A continuous bleep announces to all he should leave *now*! New technologies are a real boon to those with organisational problems, weak auditory memories and time confusions. They certainly reduce my need for yellow 'post-It' notes for clients.

Indicators in points 15 and 16 focus upon sequencing and ordering. These become notorious in getting, in order, what is needed for an assignment, essay, application or plan of action. All my dyslexia clients require help with planning and organisation, or chaos (usually resulting in anxiety absences from school, college or work) follows. The sequence problem I have also witnessed at adult dyslexia meetings. Once, having delivered a short talk to a local group, I became aware that 'questions at the end' was not an option. Interruptions were deemed as acceptable, without a sequence for who was to ask the next question – because by the end many would have forgotten what they wanted to ask so had to ask the question whilst they remembered it.

The indicators in points 17 (frustration), 18 (daydreaming) and 19 (reluctance to go to school) are self-explanatory both in children and adults. If an individual with dyslexia is unable to assimilate information, or express their knowledge, then frustration is often the consequence. Again, the 'Do's and don'ts' later in this section will look at ways of avoiding frustration. The other type of response to information overload is daydreaming – this is usually in classes or lectures that have educators talking or lecturing. Individuals with dyslexia usually learn by seeing and doing. If adaptations are not made for their learning and thinking styles, the usual consequence is that they consistently fail to turn up.

Finally, indicator in point 20 is like a bright light that you cannot ignore with individuals exhibiting literacy or numeracy difficulties: it is an indicator that says to you: 'If there are literacy/numeracy difficulties in the family, look closely at the other indicators – because with an 87% genetic link, it may be a family that experiences dyslexia.'

Can your child show signs of dyslexia and not be dyslexic?

Yes. During childhood development many children will progress through what appears to the layperson as a 'dyslexic phase'. In other words, as children develop from birth to their first days at school they may well exhibit most of the indicators listed above. This should be kept firmly in mind, and seen as completely natural. This is a usual outward sign of brain maturation and cognitive development. However, parents can become confused and become worried that their child is dyslexic, when it is all a part of natural development.

For example, if a four- to five-year-old exhibits right to left writing, and/or mirror writing (b/d confusion), and /or has scrawling, untidy penmanship – this may be an impatience to start learning fast and get along with schoolwork. However, there is the problem that can exist for professionals and parents – when can we 'start to look' for indicators.

The most balanced approach is to remain aware and vigilant, particularly if there is a family history of dyslexia, early speech difficulties (especially if a speech and language therapist has been involved), co-ordination problems and if the child cannot pick up simple rhymes. Unfortunately, only when school starts can the resulting observation for indicators begin.

If support at school is put in early, if dyslexia awareness with teachers is good, and a strong teacher-parent strategy for learning is in place, then the negative consequences of dyslexia in education can be significantly reduced.

A formal assessment may not always be necessary. More important are the early strategies between teacher and child, teacher and parent, and parent and child – agreed by all parties. A formal assessment by a psychologist will be necessary if the child's dyslexia indicators are high (above 10 out of 20) and the response at school is unhelpful.

It is always important to keep in mind that dyslexia has many positives. Former clients of mine have frequently referred to the gift of dyslexia because, outside of an educational setting, individuals with dyslexia *at least* function adequately and frequently excel at specific tasks.

Signs of dyslexia in the teenage and adult group

1. Frequent spelling mistakes still occur.

2. Reading rate may remain slow, therefore reading of any text at secondary, college or university level could cause problems.

3. Copying from the blackboard can cause considerable difficulties because of inaccurate copying or by losing the place and getting the sentences muddled.

4. Note-taking can be a problem – not understanding the main points or poor spelling. Note-taking from speech is especially difficult. They may be unable to make sense of their notes later, perhaps when needed for an essay or revision.

5. The planning of essays or assignments can prove a great burden because of the problem of the sequencing of ideas, and development of arguments. Choice of words may be restricted because of inhibitions over spellings. Word retrieval difficulties may exist, i.e. substituting simple words when they cannot recall a word they know, e.g. a client who could not recall the word 'spontaneous' said 'happened at the time when least expected' a much weaker representation from an individual who was articulate with a wide ranging vocabulary.

6. Understanding questions in comprehension: examination questions can prove difficult because of the processes involved and the ways of interpreting information.

7.   In school, French is problematical. Discussion with the school would be highly recommended. As mentioned earlier, other foreign languages present fewer problems, e.g. German, Chinese.

8.   They still tire easily and need to relax, or have a change of occupation to recuperate.

9.   The level of their work, and attitude to it, can vary from excellent on one day to abysmal on another, according to how they feel.

10. Handwriting may still need attention and help.

If five out of ten of the indicators listed on pages 13-15 apply to a teenager or adult – with some other indicators as explained earlier – then the individual would be considered 'at risk' and a formal assessment should be carried out. This could be done by a specific learning difficulties tutor with an SpLD Diploma, or a chartered psychologist with knowledge of complex specific learning difficulties. Understandably, an SpLD tutor or chartered psychologist may not always be available. Therefore, following the 'Do's and don'ts' described later would be highly recommended.

A simple guide: what to look for first

If your learner has good oral ability, or is approaching average intellectual ability or above average ability, has good practical or visual/spatial skills, but struggles with written work – you should begin to look more closely at their profile.

Learning styles and thinking styles

There are three generally accepted learning styles.

- **Auditory learning style**: prefers to be taught by 'traditional' teaching methods, and learns by 'talk, chalk, write' methods. The advantages of this learning style are reliable phonetic spelling, able to sound out letters and syllables when reading, good auditory memory, good sequential skills, and able to assimilate information by listening. However, auditory learners are easily distracted by noise, e.g. external noise or someone else talking while being taught.

- **Visual learning style**: prefers learning by what they see. They can use 'a form of thought in which images generated or recalled in the mind are manipulated, overlaid, translated and associated with other similar forms, (Thomas West, 1997). A visual learner is likely to remember written words by their shape, i.e. 'it looks right' when they spell words. They like to use pictures and colours. However, their auditory memory may be weak, they are easily distracted visually, and use phonetics as a last resort when spelling or reading.

- **Kinaesthetic learning style**: has good 'hands on' practical skills, learns best from actively investigating rather than sitting back and hearing information, requires physical activities and needs to feel and move objects around. These 'doers' tend to have unreliable phonetic skills, and are easily distracted by sound/vision.

The preferred learning style for individuals in the UK tends to break down for the population as follows:

- 37% auditory learners

- 29% visual learners

- 34% kinaesthetic learners.

Of course, you can have elements of all three, but the emphasis here is *preferred* learning style.

Individuals with complex SpLDs, especially dyslexia, are frequently visual or kinaesthetic learners. Unpublished research also indicates that young offenders are most frequently kinaesthetic learners. However, we emphasise importance of 'doing' in learning; learning literacy and numeracy in practical activity, not in classrooms.

Individuals who are auditory learners are often described as left-brain or left-hemisphere dominant. Individuals who are visual and/or kinaesthetic learners are often described as right-brain or right-hemisphere dominant.

Look at diagram 1.3 and consider which skills and activities people with dominant right brains would probably be good at. Then try and do the same thing for people with left-brain dominance.

Clearly, looking at hemispheric dominance, many individuals are in the fortunate situation of 'owning' skills from both sides of their brains. However, I am very much left-hemisphere dominant and, as you will see in diagram 1.4, I am a sequential learner with the accompanying advantages. My friends and relatives remain awe-struck by my weak practical and visual skills, and also remain irritated by my lack of interest or help in practical activities.

Individuals with dyslexia tend to be right-hemisphere dominant with the accompanying advantages. However, an individual with dyslexia does not only have to deal with irritated friends and relatives who see the disadvantages of this cognitive style, but also with educators.

Diagram I.3: Hemispheric dominance

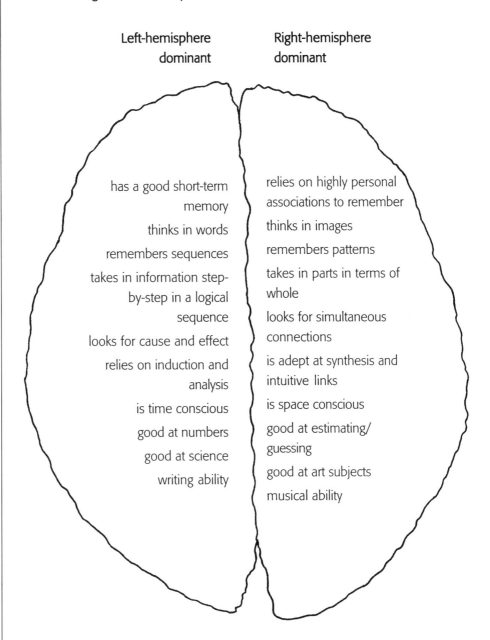

Left-hemisphere dominant	Right-hemisphere dominant
has a good short-term memory	relies on highly personal associations to remember
thinks in words	thinks in images
remembers sequences	remembers patterns
takes in information step-by-step in a logical sequence	takes in parts in terms of whole
looks for cause and effect	looks for simultaneous connections
relies on induction and analysis	is adept at synthesis and intuitive links
is time conscious	is space conscious
good at numbers	good at estimating/guessing
good at science	good at art subjects
writing ability	musical ability

Diagram 1.4

From learning styles to patterns of thinking

Likely advantages	Likely disadvantages
Good sequential memory	Accept rather than generate new ideas
Good logical planners	Tend to be regurgative
Good reading and writing skills	Unimaginative
Make steady measurable progress	Fail to make connections
Clear concept of boundaries	Unable to transfer skills
Logical thinkers	Need to plan action first
Ordered	Have difficulty making decisions without
Organised	clear evidence

Sequential learning style
(Logical, step-by-step, steady progress)

Verbal thought

Visual/kinaesthetic thought

Holistic learning style
(Learn in bursts, make connections, imaginative)
– individuals with dyslexia are likely to be in this section

Likely advantages	Likely disadvantages
Creative	Have unclear concept of boundaries
Flexible	Poor sequential memory
Good at improvisation	Poor organisation
Good at problem solving	Poor reading/writing skills
Lateral thinkers	Poor time-keeping/awareness
Good overview	Inconsistent progress
Make unusual connections	Difficult to monitor
Good visual memory	Late bloomers
Inspired	
Take risks	
Good in discussions	

Source: The Independent Psychological Service, 2003.

Therefore, both cognitive styles are equally weighted in terms of advantages and disadvantages, but the visual/kinaesthetic thinker with dyslexia will have the disadvantages impacting on educational progress, examination performance and self-esteem.

Young people I have met with dyslexia often wonder what the future holds for them. I emphasise the many areas of study and training that are available to them. Having explained to them the most beneficial ways to learn, and how they should capitalise on what they can do, I share with them the areas they might wish to consider.

Some jobs/professions/areas of study

Graphics	Novelist
Textiles	Plumbing
Art therapy	Tree surgery
Dancing	Physiotherapy
Sculpture	Personnel work
Drama	Occupational therapy
Mechanics	Care work
Gardening	Military (particularly Army)
Carpentry	Outdoor education work
Silversmithing	Medicine (e.g. surgeon)
Floristry	Racing/gambling
Music	Counsellor/politician
Reflexology	Gestalt therapist
Civil engineering	Construction work
Catering	Sport
Chef	

This list demonstrates the very wide-ranging career areas that could be considered by individuals with dyslexia. What exactly is most suitable depends (as with anyone making career choices) on that individual's particular strengths and specific difficulties.

Can you think of any more jobs?

There are clear advantages to having dyslexia! People with dyslexia tend to be:

- holistic thinkers

- good guessers

- resilient

- resourceful

- creative

- innovators

- self-reflective

- intuitive

- accurate visually and practically

- self-developing

- articulate

- often sought out to be members of a team.

Therefore, to assist young people and adults with dyslexia, it is essential to explain to them about learning styles, cognitive styles and in what areas they are more likely to bloom. Help them by visiting sites that may inspire them, and be prepared to let them try another area of learning or training if the first attempt is unsuccessful.

Further, there are important 'Dos and don'ts'.

Dos and don'ts for SpLD/dyslexia

Do:

- provide notes

- use plain type font (e.g. Century Gothic) N.B. Ask your learner what type of font they prefer

- use uncluttered, well-spaced pages

- use typeface 14

- provide relevant diagrams and pictures with brief simple wordage

- use SMOG (see Appendix)

- use coloured paper

- allow thinking time

- use multi-sensory teaching (auditory, visual and kinaesthetic)

- where possible, mark for content and knowledge

- allow use of tape or disc recorder

- give brief, specific instructions

- give overview of topic/session so learners know what to expect

- repeat instructions until remembered and understood

- assess through oral work

- wherever possible, assess practical knowledge

- revise and reinforce skills and concepts

- give extra time to work, or reduce task

- encourage use of laptop computers

- accept PowerPoint presentations

- introduce practical operations

- use video or DVD

- learn from SpLD learners – listen to them

- celebrate diversity

- obtain exam concessions

- investigate phonographix* as a teaching system for reading and spelling.

Don't:

- ask learners to copy (from white/black boards)

- use ariel type font

- use long lengths of text

- use small type face

- use only words

- use elaborate words

- use only white paper/black print

* Phonographix tutor: Alison Hopcroft, tel: 01249 891584.

- talk incessantly

- present only in auditory style

- mark for grammar and use of written language

- expect written recording

- give lengthy instructions

- begin without structure

- become irritated if asked to repeat something

- assess only in written work

- rely on words

- assume if learned once it will stick

- assume that set work is do-able

- exclude technologies that help

- only accept written essays and assignments

- exclude their best learning styles

- only teach in your preferred learning style

- assume you know best

- complain about how many learning difficulties you have to deal with

- assume individuals with SpLDs cope with written examinations

- slavishly teach basic skills.

Self help: learning strategies to cope

Below are listed some strategies a learner can adopt to help them to cope with their SpLD.

- Develop positive statements, e.g. *'I learn best when...'* as opposed to *'I can't do that...,'; 'I need more time/help to read this...'* as opposed to *'I can't read that...'; 'Can you help me to break this down into smaller chunks...'* as opposed to *'There's too much for me to do.'*

- Ask tutors/trainers or IT specialists for dyslexia (see 'Useful organisations' at the end of this book) for computer software that can help (e.g. Inspirations, Voice to Text, etc).

- If possible, obtain a palm laptop computer – there are now combined telephone and laptop (approximate cost is £300). If the learner is unable to fund themselves, or be funded by their school, college or training organisation, then they could apply to charities that might consider helping (see 'Useful organisations').

- If wishing to improve reading or spelling skills, learners can increase their use of computers for study and/or use learning systems that help basic skills (see 'Useful organisations').

- Concentrate on understanding and recording the main concepts and key points of any lectures.

- Ask for notes or handouts at the earliest opportunity. Use a tape recorder in lectures if handouts aren't available. Laptop computers can also be of use in recording information for some students.

- Use spider charts and flow charts when taking information for essays and in lectures. Keep any notes short and to the point, make them visual, learners should play to their strengths!

- Learners could, perhaps, suggest the use of video instead of a lecture on occasions.

- Keep their notes up-to-date and in good order. Perhaps use coloured pens or any other strategy to highlight the key points and concepts.

- Try using coloured acetate when reading text. Inquire about the use of coloured tinted glasses. In some cases they can be a real help (see Scotopic Sensitivity Syndrome).

- Try keeping a list of important 'things to do' in a prominent place (on the fridge); this can include main concepts from a college lecturer or something as trivial as when the newspapers need paying. This will free up short-term memory for other things. Use post-it notes or a palm laptop computer.

- Ask for extra time for assignments to be 'handed in' (if needed). Extra time and support can also be allowed even during exams.

- Inquire about other forms of presentation if they are finding it difficult. Some lecturers will allow verbal presentation.

- Talk to other dyslexics, share experiences and exchange coping skills. Learners should remember to have a laugh and a joke sometimes; it can take the pressure off work.

- Learners should not be afraid of seeking specialised help.

A key point worth noting on what has been said so far – the tutor/trainer guidelines and self-help suggestions are often relevant to the other complex SpLDs that I will address shortly. I cover these other SpLDs only relatively briefly, because much of the relevant information has already being provided. Also, as mentioned earlier, many aspects of addressing SpLDs do not need to be complex. The more effort educators expend to change the learner, the harder the job. Effort is often best expended by upskilling tutors, changing the environment and encouraging the learner's learning and thinking styles.

Section 2
Scotopic Sensitivity Syndrome

This is also referred to as Irlen Syndrome (named after Helen Irlen, who highlighted the condition) or Visual Discomfort or Light Sensitivity. To avoid further label confusion, I will refer to this paradigm as Scotopic Sensitivity Syndrome (SSS).

SSS is a visual perceptual condition that mainly affects reading and writing-based activities. It is neurologically based, and specifically affects the visual cortex's lateral geniculate bodies. Basically it is a faulty message of information sent from the back of the eye to the brain area responsible for vision: the impulse for light is inconsistent resulting in visual distortion and discomfort. It is not a fault at the front end of the eye, e.g. the lens; individuals may have perfect eyesight with SSS. However, before SSS is considered, individuals should have an eye test from a state-registered optician or optometrist.

Individuals with SSS put more energy and effort into the reading process because they are inefficient readers who see the printed page in a slightly (or severely) distorted form. The distortions can vary: visual effects that make the words on the page crush together and give the effects of white worms or rivers running down the page. When I lecture on this specific effect, I frequently hear people say *'But I thought everyone saw the page like that'* before going on to explain how reading is slow and uncomfortable, and how their reading rate and reading comprehension is affected.

Another visual effect of SSS is a spiral effect: the words on the page begin to move in a spiral, as if they were water going down a plughole. I experience this scotopic effect after approximately 12 minutes of reading – I have mild SSS. I used to think it was the drink! What a relief to find a further reason for my visual distortions. While I am writing, I am wearing blue tinted spectacles which:

(a)   reduce page glare

(b)   provide a fluency of reading and writing I lacked for decades

(c)   stop discomfort I have always experienced with words

(d)   make me look cool!

Constant adaptation to distortions from print or white background caused me fatigue and discomfort, resulting in my falling asleep while reading, or frequently having to leave my seat when working on reports or manuscripts. I think relatives and friends believe my drink problem is now slowly improving, or maybe they think the dark glasses have helped me. I know I can now read for up to 75 minutes, comprehending the content considerably more than before. Remember, 12 minutes used to be my reading limit, and 20 minutes my writing limit... and now, look, I write books! (Very slowly, still, in the eyes of my publishers.)

Therefore, the effects of SSS limit the length of time individuals can read and maintain comprehension.

If SSS goes undetected many people may be viewed as underachievers, demotivated or having poor attitudes. Indeed, I have met clients who have developed phobias because of related scotopic effects that result in depth perception problems – both with the written word and aspects of their environment. One client who experienced severe SSS had a history of educational difficulties at school and college. He had become unable to attend his course at college because of a travel phobia. When I met him he described that, in addition to his study problems at college, he could not now get on or off buses and trains to college, and subsequently developed a fear of travelling. After getting him to describe what he saw and felt in his travelling environment, it became clear that he experienced visual distortions, particularly in daylight or bright artificial light. Distortions included doorways tilting slightly from the horizontal and vertical, gaps between a train carriage step and station platform were unclear, and heights from the bus platform to the ground were a real problem for him. Despite confident assurances from the young man's optician that he had appropriate lenses for his vision, the problems continued. However, once he acquired a dark green tint to his lenses from an Irlen Institute diagnostician*, he was not only able to read text comfortably for the first time but also suffered no further distortions in his travel environment. One of his parting remarks to me was *'I could throttle you for keeping me up so late at night – I stay up late now to read all those books I couldn't read before. By the way, I can now see green leaves on trees – before they were just blobs above me.'*

Is SSS a learning difficulty?

No, not in the accepted sense. It is a complete and variable condition. It often co-exists with other learning difficulties. It can be found in combination with dyslexia, dyspraxia, dyscalculia, Attention Deficit Disorder or hyperactivity. SSS can remain undetected by standard visual and medical examinations, or psychological and educational assessments and tests. Therefore, knowledge of assessing and observing SSS is essential.

What can aggravate SSS and make the condition feel worse?

- Lighting, particularly fluorescent lighting. Lighting effects and discomfort can vary – some individuals are sensitive to cloudy days when the sun is trying to break through cloud cover, others are sensitive to sunshine, computer-screen luminance, or all of them. The discomfort can lead to migraine and headaches.

*see 'Useful organisations'

- Contrast from one lighting effect to another.

- Print size and style (closer-typed print increases severity).

- Demands for comprehending written test, when more time is needed.

- Demands for continuous performance, when there is a need for rest periods to recuperate.

It is important to note that light-sensitive migraine sufferers and epilepsy sufferers report similar problems to individuals who experience SSS.

Are there different levels of severity of SSS?

Yes, ranging from mild to severe. Mild cases usually remain undiagnosed. Visual distortions may not be noticeable until a specific tracking activity (e.g. reading) has been active for ten minutes or more. Many people may not read for that long, or claim that they find 'reading boring' (it is boring when you can no longer comprehend or assimilate what you are reading).

Moderate SSS (often occurring after five minutes into a tracking activity) can also remain undiagnosed, and can be misinterpreted as dyslexia (it is not), or Attention Deficit Disorder (it can certainly be a contributory factor).

Severe SSS, often occurring immediately when print is presented on paper, is linked with other significant symptoms affecting vision, perception and mood. Again it can be undiagnosed or misdiagnosed as poor motivation, behavioural problems or attention deficit.

Imagine this – a pupil is (again) trying to read a subject text in the classroom. The pupil is well known for lack of cooperation in academic subjects. She is experiencing problems reading the text book. The teacher tries to help:

'Remember what I've said before, if you can't read the word, sound out the first letter, then break the word down into chunks.' The teacher is taken aback with the torrent that follows from the pupil: 'And as I've told you before, I can't do it – and if you ask me to do it again, I'll tell you **again** I won't do it, now leave me alone.' What the teacher may not know, is that pupil cannot *see* the *first* letter to sound it out, never mind the 'chunks' (syllables) that follow. If the text is distorting, it will be at least difficult to read, at most impossible to read. The pupil is perceived by the teacher as uncooperative and rude; the teacher is perceived by the pupil as uncaring and unaware. Both are left with nowhere to manoeuvre. How could the situation have been different?

If the teacher had been aware of SSS he could have asked specific questions. First, 'What do you **feel** like when trying to read the text?' 'What do the words look like when you are trying to read?' 'What is it that stops you reading?' 'Do the words stay still on the page, or do they move around?' Further, the teacher would have been more aware of how to plan, organise and present written text to the class.

What are the dos and don'ts for SSS?

Where possible:

- incorporate adequate spacing

- double spacing, frequent paragraphs

- selective use of bold and bullet points

- increase usage of relevant diagrams and charts, thus cutting down the bulk of text, especially helping visual learners

- increase use of pictograms and graphics, thus assisting with the location of information

- aim for a clear, uncluttered appearance.

Avoid:

- bright white or shiny paper

- unusual or stylised fonts and italics

- printing in either green or red

- small fonts (below size 12)

- printing whole words and phrases in capitals

- busy, overcrowded pages

- assuming that one colour of paper suits all – however, recycled or beige colour paper is the most friendly generally.

Subsets of individuals

- 12–14% of the general population experience SSS.

- Up to 20% of the population experience light sensitivity, visual discomfort or SSS.

- 46% of individuals identified with learning difficulties experience SSS.

- 45–50% of individuals identified with attention deficit disorders experience SSS.

Further ways to help

- **Adjustment or modification of lighting** – medical research (Medical Research Council, University of Cambridge, New Mexico School of Medicine) has shown, by using medical physics brain scanning, that light frequencies of colour change from person to person. For some, the frequencies come too quickly or too slowly – filters and lenses* adjust the frequencies and normalise them. If I am teaching a group of people, I check what lighting levels suit the group best, and adjust lighting or seating to accommodate individual differences – otherwise up to 20% of my group may be visually distracted or discomforted.

- Provide opportunities for **regular study breaks**, especially if it involves reading or looking at a computer screen. Many individuals benefit from changing the background colour on computer screens, or providing a colour filter over the screen.

- Provide **tinted filters** or **tinted lenses**. Details of specialist optometrists and Testing Kits are available from: Cerium Visual Technologies, Cerium Technology Park, Appledore Road, Tenterden, Kent. Tel: 01580 765211. Coloured acetates, assessments and lens prescriptions are available from: Patricia Clayton, Irlen Diagnostician, Irlen South West, 123 High Street, Chard, Somerset TA20 1QT. Tel: 01460 65555.

- Watch what you **wear** (neutral colours are advised – pinstripes move!).

- Watch out for **patterns** on chairs, carpets, walls or floors.

- **Beige** and **grey** colours are generally preferred.

- Recycled paper has less glare than white.

So, before you expect individuals to listen to you when you speak, be aware that there is a lot more than just auditory information hitting sensory channels.

* Some individuals with SSS benefit from use of coloured acetates (different coloured plastic sheets on page), others benefit from coloured lenses on spectacles. My mild SSS effects are managed by adjusting lighting levels, unless I am working for more than 10 minutes on reading work, then I will use my tinted spectacles. This will vary from individual to individual – severe SSS will require lens wearing most of the time.

Section 3
Attention Deficit Disorder (ADD/ADHD)

This area of complex specific learning difficulties is probably the most controversial of all. This is not the place to discuss the many different issues surrounding the ongoing debate. I would just like to say that I do believe there is a group of young people (and adults) who meet the clinical criteria for ADD/ADHD, and a small proportion of that group do benefit from clinical intervention through prescribed medication. (The ADHD group have Attention Deficit with Hyperactivity Disorder; the ADD group have Attention Deficit Disorder without hyperactivity.)

However, I remain highly dubious about the huge increase in diagnosis in the UK, and more disturbingly in the USA where one in 12 children is now medicated to assist their schooling. In my experience, modification of curriculum and diet, improved behaviour management with counselling and personal/social skills training can substantially improve many young peoples' lives and long-term outcomes without recourse to medication.

With these qualified statements in mind, I turn to the young people I frequently meet with ADD/ADHD.

Characteristics of ADD/ADHD in young people

The vast majority of individuals I meet with an ADD/ADHD diagnosis are male. This coincides with the ratios quoted in journals and books, with males being anywhere from four to nine times more likely than females to have a diagnosis. Compared to ADD/ADHD females, males with the disorder tend to be more aggressive, impulsive and disruptive than their female counterparts. However, females tend to be under-identified and are therefore under-served, leading to greater risks for long-term academic, social and emotional difficulties.

The prevalence of ADD/ADHD is estimated to be 3–10%, again depending on the journals, books or the author's county of origin, i.e. USA estimates are generally higher than UK estimates. I favour the 4–5% estimates.

The primary characteristics found in children with Attention Deficit Disorder, namely inattention, impulsivity, and hyperactivity, are exhibited by all children to some degree. What characterises ADD/ADHD children from the other 95% of children, is that these characteristics are prevalent to a greater degree, in a wider range of social contexts and circumstances, than would be true of children without the disorder.

Inattention

This means moving from one activity to another, unable to stay focused long enough to finish an assignment, and beginning more things than those that are completed. Often distracted by noise, other external stimuli, or their own internal thoughts.

However, when engaged in enjoyable activities (computer games, skateboarding) there is a huge supply of attention. New or exciting projects or situations can capture attention for extended periods of time. Also, in one-to-one opportunities, attention span can seem normal.

Impulsivity

This relates to impulse control. This leads to racing through an activity without checking the requirements, shouting out above others in a group, losing personal possessions and equipment, and even damaging equipment. Often these things are not done maliciously, but unthinkingly. All of this can lead to a loss of friendships, with no understanding as to why, and a knack of getting on everyone's nerves.

Hyperactivity

Not all Attention Deficit Disorder individuals are hyperactive. Many show normal activity levels, or may be under-active. However, you will not miss the hyperactive ones.

Fortunately, hyperactivity is at its worst in young children. As hyperactive children get older, they tend to slow down. Unfortunately, many have – by that stage – found themselves excluded from mainstream opportunities, perhaps with some involvement with youth justice or mental health.

Hyperactive girls may express their energy in less physical ways than boys, primarily through non-stop talking.

As the ADD/ADHD individual enters and progresses through teenage years, characteristics of hyperactivity may give way to less obvious signs, e.g. tapping pencil, wagging foot, excessive talking. However, hyperactive teenagers like to keep busy, although they can have trouble settling down to the rhythm of other teenagers.

ADD without hyperactivity

There is a defined group of young people who have attention deficits but who are not hyperactive or impulsive. They account for approximately 30% of the ADD/ADHD group.

ADD individuals tend to be under-active rather than over-active. They have a slow tempo in completing tasks, and become over-focused on their own thoughts. At school, they are often described as daydreamers, confused, sluggish and lethargic. This group have a higher rate of learning problems than the ADHD group. They are more likely to develop emotional difficulties related to depression, anxiety and low self-esteem. Their peer acceptance level tends to be higher than their ADHD counterparts, but they usually remain on the periphery of a social group. Their specific difficulties tend to be with attention, motivation and organisation.

ADD/ADHD and learning difficulties

Individuals with Attention Deficit Disorder have a greater likelihood of having other specific learning difficulties, behaviour problems and social/emotional issues.

The most frequent weaknesses tend to be when using and understanding spoken or written language. Further, current research has found that ADD/ADHD children in UK, USA and Australia have at least one systematic failure in non-verbal skills, e.g. understanding/expressing tone of voice, expressing/understanding body posture, reading faces, etc (see, also in this series, Lombard, 2004, *Social Competence: reading other people*).

Estimates of learning difficulties with Attention Deficit Disorders varies from 43–92%. However, in my 25 years of working with vulnerable young people, all the ADD/ADHD individuals I have met have had a specific difficulty interpreting people in one area of non-verbal skills, with at least one deficit in the following areas: reading, writing, spelling and arithmetic.

However, I remain critical of other behaviour disorder labels linked to ADD/ADHD. Labels such as Conduct Disorder (CD) merely describe someone who behaves badly towards others and property. My belief is that by addressing effectively the needs of an individual with ADD/ADHD then CD will not be present. If, after multiple interventions that have been unsuccessful with an individual with ADD/ADHD, then it is time to re-examine the diagnosis, rather than merely adding an unhelpful label.

What an ADD/ADHD individual may feel

- Worried that they will not be able to follow the instructions, or write down the ideas in their head, or get all their work finished, or that they will be annoying to their educators/trainers and peer group.

- Embarrassed that their work does not look as nice or is 'not as good as' most of their peer group. Sometimes, their work is destroyed or hidden because of their self-consciousness.

- Frustrated that they are not able to control their behaviours and moods, and anxious about losing track, day-dreaming, opting out and needing to move around.

What ADD/ADHD people may have trouble doing

- Coping with details or a series of instructions.

- Ascertaining the mood or emotion someone may be feeling. Sometimes you have to tell them what emotion you feel because they may not recognise it.

- Choosing the right piece of information on which to concentrate and staying focused for the right amount of time.

- Planning and organising work.

- Talking and acting impulsively – tending to speak or act without taking time to consider the consequences of their actions (but regretting their actions later).

What you can do to help

- Consider the physical set-up of a room, and the ADD/ADHD individual in that room. What can be opened, may be opened. What can be touched, may be touched. Studios are better environments than classrooms.

- Divide work into small tasks with a break in between.

- Allow 'breathing space', i.e. a chance to move outside the work environment for a break.

- Use plenty of genuine positive reinforcement (smiles, thumbs up).

- Create a 'buddy' (or 'guardian') system, i.e. someone with street cred or influence to look out for him/her.

- Establish a code system with the ADD/ADHD individual to avoid verbal confrontation, e.g. to focus on work, perhaps switch on a light to gain attention; put the individual's name at the start of the sentence and gain eye contact then give a brief verbal instruction; to stop talking, signal a subtle salute, etc. (All codes should be previously discussed and agreed upon.)

Remember – do not:

- nag

- transplant insight ('Oh, I see/know what you mean...')

- lecture (too much talking and too much emotion will ruin any plan)

- argue.

Question: How do you negotiate with a hostile, out of control teenager?

Answer: You don't! Separate issues into two categories:

1.   non-negotiable issues – bottom-line rules for living in a civilised society

2.   negotiable rules – everything else! (these can be discussed as they arise, and will help form an individualised programme).

Remember – do:

- Make an appointment to discuss matters. Dealing with difficult and confrontational issues there and then will lead to catastrophe. When matters boil up, find a way out for the individual, to be discussed later.

- Speak succinctly, then leave without a display of emotion.

Ideally, ADD/ADHD individuals will be given a varied diet of activities that expend their energy, that are rarely classroom-based but frequently in studios, workshops or outside. They should be engaging with novel and creative opportunities, including social competency training (see Lombard, 2004, *Social Competence: reading other people*), counselling and relaxation training (e.g. biofeedback technology*) – and you should accept that each setback (minor and major) is a learning exercise for you and the individual.

Less ideally, the ADD/ADHD individual will be in a classroom. What follows are some guidelines addressing common complaints from teachers of ADD/ADHD students.

Talking excessively

- The teacher needs to establish rules in the classroom concerning when talking to others is acceptable or not. Some students are not able to decide when talking is appropriate, especially if students are working together on an exercise.

* Contact The Independent Psychological Service for biofeedback training

- Discuss with the talkative student why talking is inappropriate at certain times.

- At the beginning of a lesson give the student a signal when it is time to be quiet.

- Establish a consequence for unacceptable talking and apply the rule consistently to all students who break the rule, e.g. sitting on a chair near you. *Do not* use 'losing leisure time or break time' as a consequence- these individuals often need to burn off some energy.

- If you notice a student talking, first try to praise a nearby student for working quietly.

- If the student continues to talk, issue a gentle warning.

- If the student stops then continues talking, provide one of your 'consequences'.

Calling out in class

- During transition from one activity to another, let students know what is expected of them.

- Establish an agreed signal indicating permission to speak.

- Ignore students who call out without an agreed signal for permission to talk, e.g. hand raised.

- Verbally praise students who raise their hands before talking.

- Quickly call students who have raised their hands.

- Positively acknowledge hand raising, e.g. *'Jamie, you've raised your hand – what is the answer?'*

Forgetting equipment

- Teachers will often need the help of parents – emails and texts can aid parental reminders.

- The individual should remain responsible for bringing the necessary items, aided with reminders (post-it notes, mobile phone alarm).

- Request that students' parents review each evening and morning what materials are required for the next day.

Off-task during lessons

- Accept that the inattentive student may require more reminders to pay attention; sitting close to the teacher may always be necessary.

- Break assignments up in small, manageable chunks and comment on the effort made as well as the quality.

Poor listening skills

- Greet the ADD/ADHD student on arrival.

- Try to involve them in the lesson.

- Use their name with other students' names to get their attention.

- Make parts of the lesson relevant to their interests and experiences.

- Make frequent eye contact.

- Ask questions more often than others to keep them engaged.

Accept that assignments may need special attention, and the amounts may need to be modified and reduced. Highlight the positive aspects of any work handed in. Emphasise effort taken, and only compare student's progress with previous attempts – do not make comparisons with the rest of the class if self-confidence remains low.

And finally...

Evolutionary psychology can help us to understand how learning differences could well have been a part of deliberately evolved skills and abilities to enable the tribe to survive and progress. Before written language became so important in the last hundred years, individuals with dyslexia would have been recognised for what they could do – practical, creative, inspired – without having to prove they could write about it.

Individuals with ADD/ADHD may well have evolved with less dopamine (dopamine is one of our biochemicals responsible for aiding attention and controlling impulsiveness). Having less dopamine often increases physical activity. In other words, a proportion of the human tribe will have biochemically evolved over centuries as more active individuals. Therefore, such individuals were not trusted to be on sentry duty or given jobs that required attention to detail. However, as scouts, hunters and risk-takers they served a key purpose in the tribe's survival. As societies became more industrialised, they were the productive employees – perhaps not popular for accuracy, but renowned for commitment, courage and boundless energy, which often later was recognised as creative talent in the twentieth century. Until, of course, practical elements left the curriculum, apprenticeships disappeared, and classroom-based knowledge came to the fore. Coincidently, this corresponds with the same time in educational history that hyperactivity and attention problems became major players in classroom management.

With this in mind, when I meet my new intake of ADD/ADHD individuals, I aim to:

- keep them active and busy

- provide them with varied opportunities in different contexts

- enable movement by introducing them to studios and workshops

- generate interest and curiosity by providing novel activities

- provide support for weaknesses, by training in new skills, e.g. learning PowerPoint in order to record the knowledge they have and present what they know as an alternative to a written essay

- challenge them to new heights, e.g. helping me to give lectures to professionals

- help them to learn social competencies, to be accepted by a wider range of people

- address their non-verbal weaknesses, e.g. learning how others use tone of voice.

One of my late friends, Professor Bernard Watson, was notorious for his busy schedules, including 12 simultaneous research projects that were ongoing in medical physics departments in the UK and USA. This, despite being in 'retirement'. His energy was boundless. Bernard's wife said to me, shortly before his death, that he had always moved faster than a bullet and could not settle on one thing at a time. Only after reading a book on ADHD did she realise that Bernhard's chequered and challenging career was a truly great achievement – he had accentuated his impulsiveness, short attention span and high levels of activity with a truly impressive intellect. Can we not guide more of these highly evolved beings to levels they can achieve? The alternative is to concentrate only on the disordered aspects of their conduct: their response to being imprisoned in classrooms without excitement, risk-taking and novel adventures.

Section 4
Dyspraxia

Imagine you have an appointment at an office in the centre of a large city for 9am. You have not visited the city before, and it's now 8.55am. Unable to find a parking space, you drive your car into a multi-storey car park and find a space at the top level. You get out of your car, look at your watch and it's 8.59am – you do not know where the office is for your appointment, and now you start the journey to look for it.

That is how a young adult described dyspraxia to me. For her, it was like that every part of the day; knowing what she should do, but disoriented and not able to plan and organise a course of sequential actions. Worse still, despite all the expended effort, she would be greeted with the usual negativity for arriving late and perceived as disorganised.

Many of the young men I have met describe themselves as being 'in the wrong place at the wrong time' – and subsequently suffering the consequences.

Dyspraxia is occasionally referred to as clumsy child syndrome – but this outdated description overlooks the other factors that can interfere with daily life.

What is dyspraxia?

Dyspraxia is a difficulty with planning and carrying out complex movement.

Its primary effects are:

- **movement** – poor posture and balance, poor manipulation, frequently poor handwriting skills

- **language** – speech sound and order difficulties

- **perception** – difficulties in judging heights and distances; problems with copying

- **thought** – difficulties in organising and sorting out one's own thoughts; memory problems.

Secondary effects of dyspraxia are:

- **learning** – may be able to do one task one day, but not the next

- **self-esteem** – low self-esteem leading to a lack of motivation

- **initiative** – worried to try new or difficult tasks; again poor motivation

- **emotional/behavioural** – may appear stubborn and unreasonable with a strong sense of 'I know best' (this is usually developed from the experience that others don't know what's best for someone with dyspraxia).

How to help

- **assessment** – this is essential for recognition of needs, planning of education and core programmes, and entitlements (benefits and concessions). This will require assessments from a speech and language therapist, a psychologist and an occupational therapist. First port of call is the GP.

- **counselling** – an individual who experiences such a variety of confusions, frustrations and challenges through the day, requires a type of 'debrief', i.e.

'How did the day go?', 'What went well, what didn't?', 'What can be done to improve tomorrow?', 'What do you need to get ready?', 'Who might be able to help you with tomorrow's activities?'

- study planning

    – help to break down tasks into smaller, manageable steps

    – show good examples of what is required, so that the individual has a template of what to follow.

- specific strategies to overcome

    – poor manipulation: provide access to a computer, have helpers take notes; if in higher education, apply for a Disabled Student Allowance for technology and support

    – poor memory: provide handouts, copies of overhead acetates, teach mind-maps to help note-taking, help with lists and timetables, allow thinking time

    – anxiety: relaxation techniques, e.g. biofeedback*, yoga

    – poor motivation: provide assertiveness training, confidence building, social competency training.

Above all learn from these people – and celebrate diversity! They, too, are a bright group but frequently underachieve because of poor management of their needs.

Where to go for help

- **School-age children**: talk to your GP, school nurse or doctor, or special needs coordinator. Referrals for assessments can be made through your GP, school or medical officer.

* Biofeedback training available from The Independent Psychological Service (see 'Useful organisations')

- **Adults:** initial contact through the GP, who may refer to a clinical psychologist, consultant neurologist, physiotherapist or an occupational therapist.

The future

The prognosis is usually positive. Although dyspraxia is not curable, the individual may improve in many areas with developmental maturity, and with access to the appropriate support.

There is no known cause for dyspraxia. The Dyspraxia Foundation (see 'Useful organisations') states that it may be an immaturity of neurone development in the brain rather than damage to the brain. Those with dyspraxia have no clinical or neurological abnormality to explain their condition.

Section 5
Dyscalculia

Dyscalculia, or, as it is sometimes frighteningly referred to, 'mathematical disorder', is a 'cognitive disorder of childhood affecting the ability of an otherwise intelligent child to learn arithmetic' (American Psychiatric Association). The term developmental dyscalculia is applied to those children whose arithmetical ages are definitely below average in relation to their general intellectual ability and age range. This type of specific difficulty is often missed at school, and continues to be a real problem throughout school and into adulthood.

However, problems with maths are common concerns of many (including me – maths O level at the second attempt!). Therefore, it is important to consider other possible reasons for this:

- Having a learning style different to the teacher: Hughes et al. (1997) discovered that the tendency of teachers to rely on paper and pencil computation, as opposed to hands-on type activities, can have a negative effect on students' learning. (With me, I could not cope with O level mathematics as it was primarily centred on equations, but I passed my next attempt at maths because it was a different curriculum focused on design and statistics; I could cope with visual maths – graphs, tables – but not written maths. So the curriculum had been at odds with my learning. I know of young people who can only learn maths when it is directly relevant to the practical aspects of their course or training – they learn their maths in a workshop.)

- Lack of maths experiences as a child at home.

- Different cultural backgrounds (many countries around the Pacific rim teach children number by using an abacus – an excellent usual/kinaesthetic method of understanding number – but this can be undermined by a different word-based approach to maths).

- Poor language skills, including comprehension and reading.

- Poor image of self as a maths learner (that's me, too!).

- Dyslexic-type difficulties that can interfere with sequencing, order, mental arithmetic and reversals.

Addy (2000) states that a lack of visual-motor coordination and disturbances of spatial relationships are associated with arithmetic problems. Rourke (1978) had already noted that right hemisphere visual-spatial deficits (seen as visual perception, tactile perception and visual motor ability) are those cognitive deficits most often associated with dyscalculia. However, dyscalculia is likely to be the result of left- or right- hemisphere dysfunctions.

Addy (2000) examined areas responsible for perceptual processing to see why this is:

Left-hemisphere dysfunction	Right-hemisphere dysfunction
<ul><li>inability to recognise and produce number and operator symbols</li><li>mental arithmetic disturbed by poor sequencing skills</li><li>weak short-term auditory memory</li><li>dyslexia is often a feature</li></ul>	<ul><li>profound inability to conceptualise number quantity</li><li>dyspraxia</li><li>poor development of visual-spatial skills</li><li>poor development of visual-motor skills</li><li>sensory inattention</li><li>absence of stereoscopic vision</li></ul>

Source: Addy, 2000.

Assessment of dyscalculia

1. Standardised assessment:

- Wide Range Achievement Test, Third Edition (WRAT-3), arithmetic assessment

- Gardner Test of Visual Perceptual Skills (TVPS)

- Beery Test of Visual Interrogation (TVI).

  These can be obtained from The Psychological Corporation, Harcourt Education, Halley Court, Jordan Hill, Oxford OX2 8EJ. Tel: 01865 888188.

2. Non-standardised assessment

Tick each of the areas that best describe the individual. If 9 out of 11 areas are ticked, it is likely the individual is at risk of dyscalculia.

Dyscalculia symptoms

- **Normal or accelerated language acquisition**: verbal, reading and writing. Poetic ability. Good visual memory for the printed word. Good in the areas of science (until a level requiring higher maths skills is reached), geometry (figures with logic not formulae) and creative arts.

- **Difficulty with the abstract concepts of time and direction**. Inability to recall schedules, and sequences of past or future events. Unable to keep track of time. May be chronically late.

- **Mistaken recollection of names**. Poor name/face retrieval. Substitute names beginning with same letter.

- **Inconsistent results in addition, subtraction, multiplication and division.** Poor mental maths ability. Poor with money and credit. Cannot do financial planning or budgeting. Cheque books not balanced. Short-term, not long-term financial thinking. Fails to see big financial picture. May have fear of money and cash transactions. May be unable to mentally figure change due back, the amounts to pay for tips, taxes, etc.

- When writing, reading and recalling numbers, these **common mistakes** are made: number additions, substitutions, transpositions, omissions and reversals.

- **Inability to grasp and remember** math concepts, rules, formulae, sequence (order of operations), and basic addition, subtraction, multiplication and division facts. Poor long-term memory (retention and retrieval) of concept mastery – may be able to perform maths operations one day, but draw a blank the next! May be able to do book work but fails all tests and quizzes.

- **May be unable to comprehend or 'picture' mechanical processes.** Lack 'big picture/ whole picture' thinking. Poor ability to 'visualise or picture' the location of the numbers on the face of a clock, the geographical locations of states, countries, oceans, streets, etc.

- **Poor memory for the 'layout' of things.** Gets lost or disoriented easily. May have a poor sense of direction, loses things often and seems absent-minded. (Remember the absent-minded professor?)

- **May have difficulty grasping concepts of formal music education.** Difficulty sight-reading music, learning fingering to play an instrument, etc.

- **May have poor athletic coordination**, difficulty keeping up with rapidly changing physical directions like in aerobic, dance and exercise classes. Difficulty remembering dance step sequences and rules for playing sports.

- **Difficulty keeping score during games,** or difficulty remembering how to keep score in games, like bowling, etc. Often loses track of whose turn it is during games, such as cards and board games. Limited strategic planning ability for games, like chess.

The assessment also needs to explore:

- understanding of spatial concepts

- understanding of sequences

- poor short-term memory

- understanding mathematical symbols by:

  - listening to the individual reading symbols out loud

  - presenting tasks with written symbols for individual to carry out

  - asking for symbol to be written down when presented orally

- laterality – evidence of mixed laterality, or confusion over left/right direction

- understanding of shape and space

- estimations and approximations

- concentration span

- hand-eye coordination

- figure-ground discrimination.

Instructional methods to help dyscalculia (Addy, 2000)

- To help with **spatial concepts**:

  - check, then help, with understanding concepts such as under, through, opposite, in-between

  - if understanding of spatial concepts does not yet exist, it may help to physically place the individual in each of these spatial positions to gain an understanding, and then reinforce the concepts on subsequent sessions.

- **Mathematical language** is so often confusing. Sometimes, many words describe the same thing, e.g.

  - add can also mean 'total', 'the sum of', 'combine'

  - subtract can mean 'take away', 'remove', 'difference'

  - multiply can mean 'times', 'product of', 'squared'

  - divide can mean 'shared', 'over', 'between'.

Therefore, it is essential we use the same consistent term throughout instruction and conversation – until the concept is fully assimilated. Then, another term can be introduced.

Other terms, like the word 'unit' could represent 'kitchen units' in an individual's understanding, or 'x' (for times) meaning a kiss! Therefore, the consistent use of mathematical language should be used, not only by one instructor, but by a department and an organisation.

- **Understanding space** – this can include the incorrect arrangement of numbers in a computation, place value difficulties, denominations, shapes and sizes. Therefore, careful consideration should be given to the organisation of a page, e.g. bold numbers, well spaced, with a clear colour coding, e.g. units (red), tens (black), hundreds (green); specific colours for specific shapes, e.g. squares are red, rectangles are blue. Also, do not assume that an individual knows the difference between a square (2D) and a cube (3D). The concepts of 2D and 3D may need to be taught.

- **Estimations/approximations** – a useful exercise to help with understanding the concept of varying quantity. Use of visual images for guessing number, and guesstimates of numbers using a calculator, and general guide guesses with money (change, pay, etc.) can help strengthen this skill. If times tables are not known, techniques can be taught, e.g. nine times table:

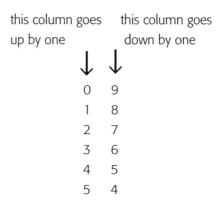

this column goes up by one ↓

this column goes down by one ↓

0	9
1	8
2	7
3	6
4	5
5	4

- **Laterality** – awareness of left-to-right orientation (as in reading) and right-to-left (as in calculating). Help can be given by:

  - providing a starting point by a colour, e.g. yellow = left to right, orange = right to left

  - drawing letters or numbers on an individual's back, and asking what letter/number it was

  - numbers in the air

  - activities on the importance of columns (all types!), importance of columns for the decimal point (£500 is different from £5)

  - activities related to rotation, e.g. clock faces, angles, compass points.

- **Understanding the form of number** – if reversals still occur, e.g. 3/5, 6/9, then work only with numerals in specific groups until they are correctly formed, e.g. only work with numerals 1, 2, 3 until 3 is correctly formed, before introducing 4, 5, 6 – then make sure 6 is correctly formed before introducing 7, 8, 9 and 10.

  - provide calculators at **all** times

  - use measuring rods, rulers

  - always have a visual/kinaesthetic approach when working with numbers

  - always use colour.

- **Figure-ground discrimination** – many individuals with dyscalculia have real difficulty when there is an overload on the visual senses. Many modern textbooks are colourful, wordy, with different type sizes and form. To help those with dyscalculia, information should be restricted, e.g. one sum or piece of information at a time. This may require pages of textbooks being photocopied, cut up and stuck separately onto pages.

- **Fine motor skills** – often, individuals are discouraged from using their fingers when they count. Individuals with dyscalculia should not be discouraged. Finger counting is a learned method to help them 'see' the numbers.

- **Understanding sequences** – through overlearning, individuals with sequencing difficulties are able to learn popular sequences by counting forwards, but remain unable to count backwards sequentially. Help individuals to sequence by practising forwards/backwards in:

  - days of the week

  - months of the year

  - pattern work.

Also, giving opportunities in:

- simple jigsaws, progressing to more difficult

- following recipes.

- **Poor short-term memory** – to give help with improving short-term memory problems:

 - limit the number of sequences within instructions

 - use a multi-sensory approach: verbal – practical – written – audio/ video taped sequences of instructions

 - limit time spent on a subject to avoid overload.

- **Attention span** – in order to maintain concentration:

 - ensure work is at an appropriate age level

 - revisit previous topics/work/skills

 - give time, and individualise programmes

 - although there is a need for over-learning, beware of 'motivational burnout'.

Dyscalculia is not only a problem with number or maths. It is often a wider-ranging cognitive style, with weaknesses in sequencing, memory shape and space, laterality and hand-eye coordination. Therefore, any approach will require a programme to assess and address these needs. One qualification programme I have used, combined with an individualised remedial programme, is the City and Guilds 3750 Numeracy course. The multiple choice examination reduces some of the sequential problems that an individual may experience. If this course is replaced, look for one that (a) looks at each arithmetic skill in graduated level of difficulty, (b) provides a method of assessment that reduces the need for lengthy calculations or formulae and (c) provides a form of assessment that is multiple choice or brief answer.

Useful organisations

ADDISS (The National Attention Deficit Disorder Information and Support Service) – 10 Station Road, Mill Hill, London NW7 2JU. Tel: 020 8906 9068. www.addiss.co.uk email: info@addiss.co.uk

Adult Dyslexia Organisation – Tel: 020 7924 9559. email: dyslexia.hq@dial.pipex.com

British Dyslexia Association – 98 London Road, Reading RG1 5AU. Tel: 0118 966 2677. www.bda-dyslexia.org.uk email: admin@bda-dyslexia.demon.co.uk

City & Guilds of London Institute – 1 Giltspur Street, London EC1A 9DD. Tel: 020 7294 2000. www.city-and-guilds.co.uk email: enquiry@city-and-guilds.co.uk

Disability on the Agenda – FREEPOST, Bristol BS38 7DE.

For information on dyscalculia see: www.dyscalculia.org

Dyslexia Computer Research Centre – Department of Psychology, University of Hull, Hull HU6 7RX.

Dyspraxia Foundation – 8 West Alley, Hitchin, Hertfordshire SG5 1EG. www.dyspraxiafoundation.org.uk email: dyspraxiafoundation@dyspraxiafoundation.org.uk

The Independent Psychological Service – 6 Ash Walk, Warminster, Wiltshire BA12 8PY. Tel: 01985 847134.

Irlen/Scotopic Sensitivity Syndrome – **Irlen Institute,** 5380 Village Road, Long Beach California 90808, USA.

For Irlen products, training, assessments in the UK: Patricia Clayton, **Irlen Centre South West,** 123 High Street, Chard, Somerset TA20 1QT.

SKILL (National Bureau for Students with Disabilities) – 4th Floor, Chapter House, 18-20 Crucifix Lane, London SE1 3JW. Tel: 0800 328 5050. www.skill.org.uk email: info@skill.org.uk

References

Addy, L. (2000), *Dyscalculia*, Paper presented to the Annual Conference of Professional Association of Teachers and Students with Specific Learning Difficulties, 1 April 2000.

Hughes, S., Kolstad, R., Briggs, L. (1997), *Dyscalculia and Mathematics Achievement*, Journal of Learning Disabilities, Vol. 733, 46-59.

Lombard, G. (2004), *Social Competence: reading other people,* Trowbridge: Lifetime Careers Publishing.

Rourke, B. (1978), *Reading, Spelling and Arithmetic Disabilities: A Neurological Analysis*, in H. Mykelburst (Ed.) (1978), *Progress in Learning Disabilities,* Vol. 4, New York: Guilford Press.

West, T. (1997), *In the Mind's Eye,* New York: Prometheus Books.

Appendix

SMOG readability formula – simplified

Readability is an attempt to match the reading level of written material to the 'reading with understanding' level of the reader.

This formula calculates readability using sentence and word length. However, other factors affect understanding of what you are reading that cannot be measured in this way, e.g. motivation of reader, size and type of print, layout of written material, previous knowledge of subject, style of writer, etc.

SMOG is much quicker and easier to work out by hand than other formulae.

1. select a text

2. count 10 sentences

3. count number of words which have three or more syllables

4. multiply this by 3

5. circle the number closest to your answer

    1 4 9 16 25 36 49 64 81 100 121 144 169

6.   find the square root of the number you circled

1 4 9 16 25 36 49 64 81 100 121 144 169
1 2 3 4 5   6 7 8 9 10 11   12   13

7.   add 8.

A readability level under about 10 will be able to be understood by most people.

Once you master SMOG with a bit of practice, you realise that short, regular words serve just as well as long, multi-syllable irregular words. For example:

Question: What does this mean: *'Assess and critically evaluate the brown, viscous liquid contained in the glass receptacle'?*

Answer: It means: *'How's your pint?'*

The first way the question is worded is in elaborated code, used in textbooks and examination questions. The alternative question *'How's your pint?'* is in restricted code usually used in relaxed conversation between relatives and friends. It is the restricted code (linked with visual images) I promote for practical areas of study and training.